Speaker Struggles?

Don Barnes

Published by Don Barnes, 2024.

LifeWorksInThrees.com

Table of Contents

About the Author...1

Introduction 5

My discovery of the Tryune Concept..................................8

SPEAKER... 25

KNOW 27

Study.. 29

Experience 31

Mentors... 33

PRACTICE 35

Outline... 37

Delivery 39

Critique.. 41

PRESENTING 43

Image 45

Time 47

Bonus Chapter – Joining a Speaker Club......................... 51

SUMMARY 53

Invitation 54

Other titles coming out:... 56

Quotes about Speakership 57

"Tell 'em what you're going to tell 'em. | Then, tell 'em. | And then, tell 'em what you just told 'em.".. 63

About the Author

Don is the founder and author of Life Works in Threes!™ E-books. He is a lifelong Texan who has traveled extensively while taking a keen interest in human behavior. His curiosity about life and what drives humans led him to the discovery of how life works in threes. He coined this term as the *Tryune Concept.*

Don attended college on an athletic scholarship and then embarked on a 30-year career in the oil and gas industry. Since the year 2000, he has been a consultant for distributors and manufacturers of various industries. Along the way, he worked on his Tryune discovery in hopes of someday sharing his findings with those struggling unnecessarily... in life. What Don surmised from 40+ years of R&D was that people were struggling unnecessarily because they were not aware that "life works in threes." They, for the most part, have been living their lives by chance rather than by choice, he also discovered.

From this, he began focusing on the "mechanics of life" which shows formulas for success with subjects such as *life, health, money, purpose and so forth.* When people are able to grasp the Tryune Concept, they can apply the formulas with topics that interest them and begin eliminating the struggle. This epiphany is what triggered his Tryune venture and is now on the path of sharing with all who desire to improve on their lives.

Don currently resides in Southern California and Texas while overseeing his businesses and investments.

Life Works in Threes™

When I was a kid growing up, no one sat me down and said, "Okay Don, I'm going to show you how life works so that you can navigate your way through adulthood." I graduated from school, got married and went about my way with the "learn as you go" concept. It was kind of like putting together a backyard swing set without a set of instructions. Lots of frustration and do-overs, for sure!

My discovery of the "triune" word and noticing how things come together in threes is really what set me off on researching that maybe "life comes in three" ...sort of a mechanical approach to managing life, if you will. I combed the libraries and bookstores for information on this and found one book on the subject that was written back in 1951. The author's name was John S. Arant.

What Mr. Arant had to say is this "For lack of a better name, I have called this *The Triangle of Triumph* and therefore, consistent with the name, since most of these conclusions are built on the geometric figure of the triangle." He continued "All Life and all lives are seated in, and circumscribed by, the triangle. The Author and Source and Director of all life is Himself triune in character – Father, Son, and Holy Spirit. Man is of triple nature – body, mind, and spirit – and within those three there are many triangles – desires, development, decay; intellect, will, sensibilities. Of this "paced interlude in the midst of eternity" which we call time there is the triangle of Past, Present, and Future. Space – that limitless and measureless element of the physical universe – is best known in terms of Height, Breadth, and Depth. Try building yourself some triangles along the lines of your Will, your Work, your Way – You will find some interesting angles.

So, for the first time, I realized that life is designed in a mechanical way to come in threes. That means you don't have to rely on wishing and hoping things turn out okay. You can actually look at the three parts that a particular thing is made of and then apply them to get what you're wanting. Like a three-ingredient recipe or a combination lock. With a combination lock, you need the three exact numbers to unlock the lock...otherwise you will continue to struggle.

Some 40 years later, I accumulated things that work in threes and that's when I knew I needed to share this with anyone wanting answers. To have success/harmony in your life, just apply the three parts of an area you're working on, and things will fall into place. I also learned that the recipe for success with just about anything is by doing these three things, consistently – THINK positively, SPEAK positively and ACT positively. For example, if I want to be a successful artist. I would think to myself "I can do this because I have the talent." Then I would speak it this way "Yes, I am working on my art degree and plan to do portraits professionally." Finally, I would act on that by taking art classes and continue crafting my skill. Eventually, I will see the positive results/success I'm looking for.

Conversely, if I think positively but speak negatively...it will cancel out. Or if I speak positively but have no positive action going on...nothing will happen.

I looked up "How Life Works" and "The Mechanics of Life" and these are really talking about the biology of how our cells work and other chemistry. TRYUNE WORKS! teaches that life is kind of like building blocks. Pick a topic you may be struggling with. See the three parts that topic consists of and then start applying them...on a consistent basis. That will help you overcome the struggle and get you back in harmony/success with how life works.

For 30+ years I was a golf instructor (by accident). My two kids had some success playing junior golf and so friends and neighbors would ask me to show them and their kids how to play golf successfully. From all of this, I got pretty good at watching golfers on the driving range and could spot right away why they were struggling with hitting bad golf shots. I was able to do that because I knew the three steps to hitting good golf shots. I learned them from studying golf and played for several decades. I "broke the code" for me so to speak.

So now you know that life works in threes. You can live your life *by choice* rather than *by chance* and that my friend... is the key to a fulfilling life.

Introduction

Being a polished speaker can be a game-changer in your career journey. Imagine this: whether you're pitching a new idea to your team, presenting at a conference, or simply engaging in a discussion with colleagues, the ability to articulate your thoughts clearly and persuasively can set you apart from the crowd. First and foremost, being a polished speaker enhances your communication skills. You'll find it easier to convey complex ideas in a way that everyone understands, fostering better teamwork and collaboration. This skill is invaluable in any profession, from sales and marketing to engineering and healthcare.

Additionally, polished speakers often exude confidence. When you can speak confidently about your work and ideas, others are more likely to trust and respect your expertise. This can lead to greater opportunities for career advancement and leadership roles. Moreover, being able to speak well enhances your professional presence. Whether you're networking at a conference or giving a presentation to potential clients, how you communicate reflects on your professionalism and competence. People are naturally drawn to those who can express themselves clearly and effectively, making it easier to build valuable connections and expand your professional network.

Lastly, being a polished speaker can boost your credibility and influence. When you can articulate your ideas persuasively, you're more likely to sway opinions and inspire action. Whether you're advocating for a new project, negotiating a deal, or leading a team through a challenging situation, your ability to speak with impact can make all the difference. It's not just about what you say, but how you say it that can leave a lasting impression on others. So, investing in honing your speaking skills can pay off in numerous ways throughout your career, helping you to achieve your goals and make a meaningful impact in your field.

LIFE WORKS
IN THREES!

My sanctuary on the Pacific coast

My discovery of the Tryune Concept

Before we dive into speaker struggles and how to overcome them, let me share my discovery of the Tryune Concept and how life works in threes. It all began in the summer of 1982.

I grew up with parents who treated everyone with decency and respect. My three older sisters and I were raised in a home that was "middle-class traditional." We lived in modest homes in different small towns, attended school and church on a regular basis and celebrated all the traditional holidays. Eventually we settled during the spring of 1964 in the big city of Houston, Texas. I'll never forget the vastness of the city and hearing sirens from police cars, fire trucks and ambulances on a regular basis. I was excited and scared at the same time.

Once settled in this fast-paced city, I finished my growing-up years with an academic diploma and sweetheart intact. I got a job, bought a car, got married, bought a house and produced two beautiful babies in a span of about 5 years. Talk about having to grow up fast!

Things went from great in my childhood to absolute misery in my young adulthood. I began to struggle with my job because deep down I just hated what I was doing. This problem created a snowball effect because soon after, my weight, my finances, my relationships, my happiness and everything else worth saving was going down the drain. I eventually hit a level of frustration that I had never experienced before and didn't know how to get out of it. My cry for help was for anyone or anything to come to my rescue. I just ran out of solutions for my situation.

This is when my discovery happened.

One night shortly after my meltdown, while sleeping soundly, the word "triune" began to softly pound in my head like a mantra. I woke up a little startled and decided to go look up the word in my favorite dictionary (this was WAY before Google.) The definition said '**triune** (try-une) – 1) a group of three things; united. 2) Being 3 in 1 such as *humans are mental, physical and spiritual.* I scratched my head, got a glass of water and went back to bed.

The next day while driving around town, I began thinking about things that I was taught in my younger years that came in threes. My Boy Scout manual taught that to have **character**, I needed to be *1) physically strong, 2) mentally awake and 3) morally straight.* My high school football coach would say emphatically "If you want to be **a good football player**, you have to be *1) mobile 2) agile and 3) hostile!*" My first sales manager shared with me that to be **a successful salesman**, I needed to have *1) sales skills, 2) product knowledge and 3) a good image.*

"Hmm", I thought, "wonder if there are other examples out there of things that work in threes?" So, some 40 years later, I have researched and discovered that many, many things work in threes. What this message was telling me is that to achieve success or balance in any significant area of my life, the three things that area consisted of had to be present continuously. That's when I had my epiphany. This discovery was telling me the secret to how life <u>really</u> works.

Tryune is a play on the word "triune" as an invitation to "try" this concept. Furthermore, we do not say that life <u>only</u> works in threes. Life also works in ones, twos, fours and so on. What has been observed though is that the many things significant to life, just so happen to come and work in threes. That's what is being shared in this book.

Now, you are about to see 40+ years of research and proof that life works in threes. I did not make up any of these topics. I invite you to research them on the internet to validate what is written here. There are some interesting facts that most of us have never realized...until now.

How Life Works in Threes (around 200 examples)

<u>LIFE</u>

Humans consist of *body, mind and soul.*

A human's basic needs are *health, income and provisions.*

A human's basic wants are *comfort, gain and approval.*

Our minds are made up of the *conscious, the subconscious and the unconscious.*

Philosophy explains *the id, the ego and superego.*

Atoms consist of *protons, neutrons and electrons.*

Motion is explained by *three basic laws.*

Science falls under three main branches: *natural, social and formal sciences*

Time is *past, present and future*...at the same time.

Electricity consists of *ohms, amperes and voltage.*

Music's basic elements are *duration, pitch and timbre.*

Democracy is a government *of the people, by the people and for the people.*

U.S. branches of government are *the judicial, the executive and the legislative.*

Armed Forces protect us on *land, air and sea.*

Environmentally, we are asked *to reduce, recycle and re-use.*

The news program gives us *the news, sports and conditions.*

Our days consist of *morning, afternoon and evening.*

Three months in each season of the year

Our main meals are known as *breakfast, lunch and dinner.*

A balanced diet consists of *good proteins, carbohydrates and fats.*

Traditional Family consists of *father, mother, and child(ren)*

<u>SCIENCES</u>

Three major branches of natural science – *(physical, earth/space and life sciences)*

Three major branches of modern physics - *(classical, relativistic, quantum)*

Three major branches of biology *(botany, zoology, microbiology)*

Three spatial dimensions: *height* (up/down), *width* (left/right) and *depth* (forwards/backwards)

Three-gauge bosons (photon, gluon, W&Z bosons)

Three types of elementary particles *(leptons, quarks, gauge bosons)*

Three quarks in every proton *(two "up" and one "down")*

Three primary colors of light *(red, green, blue)*

Three color tone properties *(hue, value, chroma)*

Three laws of motion (*Newton's laws*)

Three laws of planetary motion (*Kepler's laws*)

Three layers of the Sun's interior (*core, radiative zone, convective zone*)

Three layers of the Sun's atmosphere (*photosphere, chromosphere, corona*)

Three types of meteorites (*iron, stony iron, stony*)

Three types of galaxy shapes (*elliptical, spiral, irregular*)

Three substances of the universe (*normal matter, 'dark matter', 'dark energy'*)

Three phases of the moon (*new moon, first quarter, full moon*)

Three planetary regions (*temperate, sub-tropical, tropical*)

Three layers of the Earth (*crust, mantle, core*)

Three components of an ecosystem (*producers, consumers, decomposers*)

Three types of rocks (*igneous, sedimentary, metamorphic*)

Three types of fossil fuels (*coal, crude oil, natural gas*)

Three hydrological processes (*evaporation, condensation, precipitation*)

Three basic types of (meteorological) precipitation (*liquid, freezing, frozen*)

Three types of substances *(mono-constituent, multi-constituent, UVCB)*

Three phases of (normal) matter *(solid, liquid, gas)*

Three types of covalent chemical bonds *(single, double and triple bonds)*

Three isotopes of hydrogen *(protium, deuterium, tritium)*

Three atoms in each molecule of water *(two hydrogen atoms and an oxygen atom)*

Three endings to salts *(-ide, -ite, -ate)*

Three requirements for fire *(fuel, oxygen, heat)*

Three nucleotide bases in a genetic codon

Three domains of life *(archaea, bacteria and eukaryotes)*

Three major groups of flowering plants *(monocots, eudicots, magnolids)*

Three major functions that are basic to plant growth and development: *(photosynthesis* [making sugars], *respiration* [metabolizing those sugars], and *transpiration* [water vapor loss]

Three things that the chlorophyll in plants needs for photosynthesis to take place: *(sunlight, carbon dioxide and water)*

Transpiration serves three roles: *(cooling the plant, moving minerals* and *sugars through the plant,* and *maintaining the turgidity pressure* [stiffness] *of the plant's cells)*

Three parts of an insect's body *(head, thorax, abdomen)*

<u>BIOLOGY</u>

Three types of cones in the retina, relating to the three primary colors

Three semi-circular canals in the ear *(lateral, anterior, posterior)*

Three sections in the ear *(outer, middle, inner)*

Three ossicles in the middle ear *(malleus, incus, stapes)*

Three segments to each limb *(proximal, mid, distal)*

Three bones in each arm *(humerus, radius, ulna)*

Three joints in the arm *(shoulder, elbow, wrist)*

Three joints in the leg *(hip, knee, ankle)*

Three joints in the elbow *(humeroulnar, humeroradial, proximal radioulnar)*

Three functional compartments in the knee joint *(the femoropatellar, medial femorotibial* and *lateral femorotibial articulations)*

Three types of fibrous joints *(sutures, gomphoses, syndesmoses)*

Three types of bone in each hand (*carpals, metacarpals, phalanges*)

Three types of bone in each foot (*tarsals, metatarsals, phalanges*)

Three bones (phalanges) in each finger and in each toe (*proximal, intermediate, distal*)

Three layers of skin (*dermis, epidermis, hypodermis*)

Three components of a cell (*cell membrane, nucleus, cytoplasm*)

Three types of blood vessels (*arteries, veins, capillaries*)

Three types of blood cells [*red* (erythrocytes), *white* (leukocytes), *platelets* (thrombocytes)]

Three processes of the intestinal tract (*ingestion, digestion, excretion*)

Three germ layers (*Endoderm, Mesoderm, Ectoderm*)

Three parts of a human tooth (*crown, neck, root*)

Three organs of otolaryngology (*ear, nose, throat*)

Three major body systems (*digestive, circulatory, respiratory*)

Three parts to a neuron: (*soma* [*cell body*], *axon, dendrites*)

Three main parts of the brain (*forebrain, midbrain, hindbrain*)

Three parts of the forebrain *(cerebrum, thalamus, hypothalamus)*

Three parts of the midbrain *(colliculi, tegmentum, cerebral peduncles)*

Three parts of the hindbrain *(cerebellum, pons, medulla)*

Three membranes enclosing the brain *(dura mater, arachnoid, pia mater)*

The brain operates on three levels: *consciously* (for cognitive thought and declarative memory); *subconsciously* (for pre-planned actions and procedural memory); and *unconsciously* (for breathing, heart beating, etc.)

Our conscious mind is fed from three sources: *our senses* (which can be fooled); *our memory* (which is flawed); and *our imagination* (which is inventive)

Three aspects of the human mind *(memory, intellect, will)*

Three parts of the human personality *(id, ego, superego)*

The sum of human capacity consists of three abilities *(thought, word and deed)*

Three times of man *(birth, life, death)*

Three periods of the Gait Cycle *(initial double limb support, single limb support, and terminal double limb support)*

<u>MUSIC</u>

Three types of musical notes *(sharps, flats, naturals)*

Three aspects of a song (*lyrics, melody, rhythm*)

Three types of musical chords (*root, third, fifth*)

MATHEMATICS

Three types of a real number (*positive, negative, zero*)

Three parts to any arithmetic operation: for addition: *augend, addend and sum* - for subtraction: *minuend, subtrahend and difference* - for multiplication: *multiplicand, multiplier and product* - for division: *dividend, divisor and quotient*

Three laws of arithmetic operations (*commutative, associative, distributive*)

Three types of equivalence relation (*reflexivity, symmetry, transitivity*)

Three types of symmetry operations (*translation, rotation, reflection*)

Three geometries (*Euclidean, spherical, hyperbolic*)

The number 3 is the basis of an entire branch of mathematics, called trigonometry (from the Greek *trigonon* "triangle" + *metron* "measure")

Three trigonometric functions (*sine, cosine, tangent*)

Three types of average (*mean, mode, median*)

GRAMMAR

Three logical operators (*AND, OR and NOT*)

Three laws of logic (*identity, noncontradiction, excluded middle*)

Three parts of a logical syllogism (*major premise, minor premise, conclusion*)

Three grammatical parts to a sentence (*subject, verb, complement*)

Three persons in grammar [*1st person* (I/we), *2nd* (you or your), *3rd* (he/she/it/they)]

Three genders in grammar [*masculine* (he/him), *feminine* (she/her), *neuter* (it)]

Three forms of comparison in grammar [*positive, comparative* (more, -er), *superlative* (most, -est)]

Three cases in (English) grammar [*subjective/nominative* (he), *objective/accusative* (him) and *possessive/genitive* (his)]

Three parts of a narrative (*beginning, middle, end*)

Components of an essay (*introduction, body, conclusion*)

Elements of a rhetorical appeal (*ethos, pathos, logos*)

Aspects of a story (*plot, characters, setting*)

<u>RELIGION</u>

The Creator – *omniscient, omnipotent, omnipresent*

Christian God – *Father, Son, Holy Spirit*

Jesus – *The Way, The Truth, The Life*

Ancient Near East- *Qudshu, Astarte, Anat*

Classical Antiquity – Many dieties came in threes

Hinduism – Para Brahman is *Brahma, Visnu, Shiva*

Ancient Celtic Cultures – *many example of triad dieties*

Buddhism – *The three jewels*

Taoism – *The three pure ones*

Islam – *Fear, Hope and Love*

Baha'i - *Intention, Power and Action*

Confucianism – *Benevolence, Wisdom and Courage*

<u>OTHER TRIUNE EXAMPLES</u>

3 Coins in a Fountain

3 Days of the Condor

3 Miles in a League

3 Goals in a Hat Trick

3 Piece Suit

3 Feet in a Yard

3 Books in Lord of the Rings

3 Ring Circus

3 Ships of Christopher Columbus

3 Sheets to the Wind

3 Books in a Trilogy

3 Wheels on a Tricycle

3 Wise Men

3-Legged Race

3 Ring Circus

3-Wheeler

3 Cornered Hat

3 Dimensional

3 Musketeers

3 R's (reading, 'riting, 'rithmatic)

3 Sides of a triangle

3 Races in the Triple Crown (horse racing)

3 Angles in a Triangle

3 Trimesters in a Pregnancy

3 Flavors in Neapolitan Ice Cream

3 Stars in Orion's belt

3 Barleycorns in an Inch

3 Hands on a Clock (with the Seconds Hand)

3 Colors in a Flag

3 Minute Egg

3 Great Pyramids at Giza

3 Holes in a Bowling Ball

3 Colors in a Set of Traffic Lights

3 Minutes in a Boxing Round

3 Teaspoons in a Tablespoon

3 Legs on a Stool

3 Monastic Vows (Obience, Stability, Conversatio Morum)

3 Body Types: Endomorph, Mesomorph, Ectomorph

3 Ring Notcbooks

3 Germ layers: Endoderm, Mesoderm, Ectoderm

3 Species of Homo: Homo habilis, Homo erectus, Homo sapiens

3 Basic parts of a camera: Lens, Shutter, Sensor

3 Stages of a Project lifecycle: initiation, planning, execution

The Truth, The Whole Truth and Nothing but the Truth

Life, Liberty and the Pursuit of Happiness

Hear no Evil, See no Evil, Speak no Evil

National motto of France/Haiti: Liberty, Equality, Fraternity

Paper, Rock, Scissors

Ready, Aim, Fire

On Your mark, Get Set, Go

Olympic medals of gold, silver, bronze

Types of joints (ball & socket, hinge, pivot)

Stages of a rocket launch (launch, orbit, re-entry)

Parts of a joke (setup, delivery, punchline)

Primary components of a transistor (emitter, base, collector)

Primary components of an airplane (fuselage, wings, empennage)

Basic components of a computer: CPU, memory, storage

Three phases in the development of technology (*eotechnic* [*mechanical*], *paleotechnic* [*steam-powered*] and *neotechnic* [*electric-powered*]

Communication systems require three components (*transmitter, channel, receiver*)

The list goes on. See if you can find more examples as they are everywhere in our universe! Now that you know that life works in threes (with proof!), we can begin to apply this concept to whatever topics we want.

So, to overcome struggles in speakership, we need to apply the three areas that speakership consists of – KNOW, PRACTICE and PRESENTING. Let's get started!

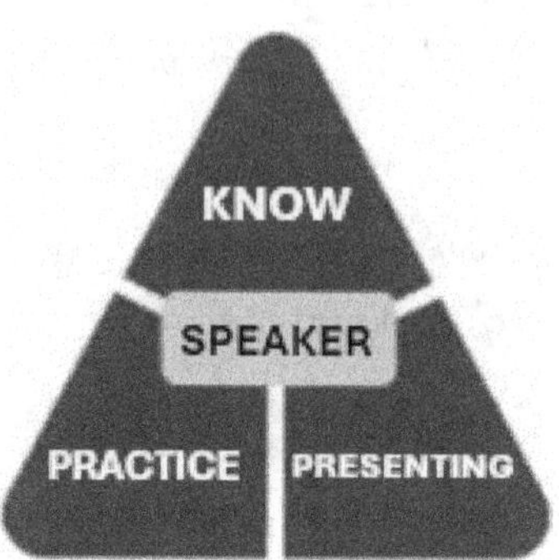
KNOW
SPEAKER
PRACTICE
PRESENTING

SPEAKER

Becoming a successful speaker can bring a wealth of rewards that extend far beyond the stage. One of the most immediate rewards is the sense of accomplishment and confidence that comes from mastering the art of public speaking. When you can captivate an audience, convey your message effectively, and receive positive feedback, it boosts your self-esteem and validates your hard work. This newfound confidence often spills over into other areas of your life, empowering you to tackle new challenges and opportunities with greater assurance.

Another rewarding aspect of being a successful speaker is the opportunity to inspire and influence others. Whether you're sharing personal experiences, advocating for a cause, or imparting knowledge, your words have the power to motivate and enlighten listeners. Witnessing the impact of your message on individuals or even larger audiences can be incredibly fulfilling. Knowing that you've made a positive difference in someone's life through your speaking engagements can be one of the most rewarding aspects of being a speaker.

Also, being a successful speaker can open doors to new professional opportunities. It can enhance your visibility within your industry or community, leading to invitations for speaking engagements at conferences, events, or workshops. These opportunities not only broaden your network but also position you as an authority in your field. Additionally, speaking engagements can lead to collaborations, partnerships, or even new business ventures as people recognize your expertise and leadership. Ultimately, the rewards of being a successful speaker are not just about personal satisfaction but also about making meaningful contributions to others and advancing your career in exciting ways.

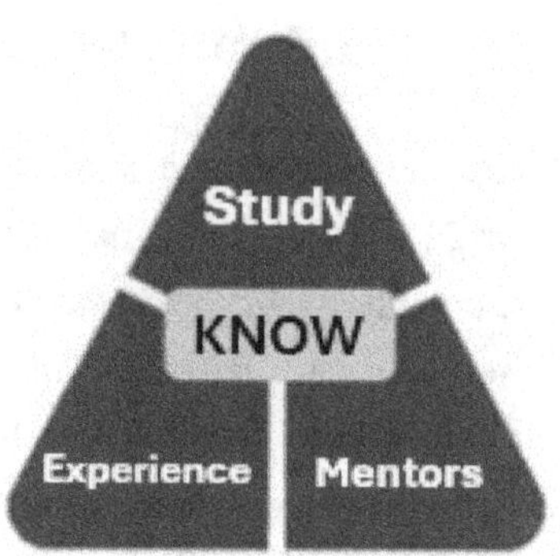
Study
KNOW
Experience
Mentors

KNOW

Knowing your topic inside and out is like having a superpower as a speaker—it's essential for delivering a compelling and credible presentation. First and foremost, when you thoroughly understand your topic, you exude confidence. You're able to speak fluently and with authority, which captivates your audience and earns their trust. This confidence isn't just about memorizing facts; it's about having a deep understanding that allows you to answer questions, address concerns, and provide valuable insights.

Additionally, knowing your topic allows you to tailor your message to fit your audience. You can anticipate their interests, concerns, and level of knowledge, which helps you to frame your information in a way that resonates with them. Whether you're presenting to experts in your field or to a general audience, your ability to speak knowledgeably and adapt your content accordingly ensures that your message is relevant and impactful.

Finally, a strong command of your topic enables you to handle unexpected situations with ease. From handling challenging questions to navigating technical difficulties, your expertise serves as a reliable anchor. It allows you to stay composed and agile, ensuring that your presentation remains engaging and informative. Ultimately, knowing your topic isn't just about delivering a speech—it's about empowering yourself to connect with your audience, deliver value, and leave a lasting impression. It's the foundation upon which successful speaking engagements are built.

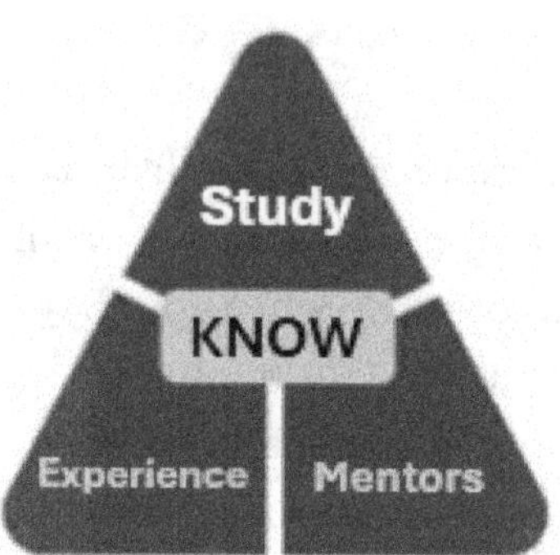
Study
KNOW
Experience
Mentors

Study

Common sense tells us that studying your topic thoroughly before a speaking engagement is like laying a solid foundation for a sturdy building—it's absolutely crucial. First and foremost, deep knowledge of your topic allows you to speak with authority and confidence. When you've taken the time to research and understand the subject matter, you can articulate your points clearly and convincingly. This not only captivates your audience but also instills trust in your expertise. Whether you're discussing complex theories or practical applications, your preparedness shines through, making your presentation more engaging and impactful.

Studying your topic enables you to anticipate and address potential questions or objections from your audience. By delving into different aspects, viewpoints, and nuances of the topic, you're better equipped to provide comprehensive answers and explanations. This fosters a more interactive and dynamic exchange with your audience, where you can enrich their understanding and encourage meaningful dialogue. Your thorough preparation demonstrates respect for your audience's time and interest, showing that you've invested effort to deliver value.

In closing, studying your topic allows you to tailor your presentation to meet the needs and expectations of your specific audience. Whether you're speaking to colleagues, clients, students, or industry professionals, understanding their background and interests helps you to customize your content effectively. This personalized approach ensures that your message resonates with your audience, making your presentation more relevant and memorable. Ultimately, studying your topic isn't just about mastering information—it's about crafting a compelling narrative that engages, educates, and inspires your listeners. It's the foundation for delivering a successful and impactful speaking engagement.

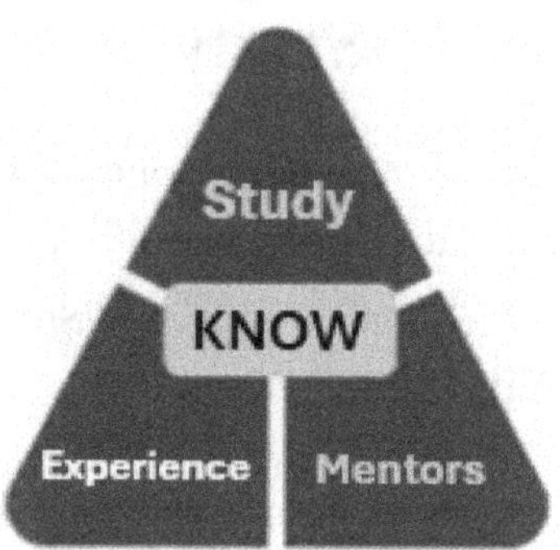
Study
KNOW
Experience
Mentors

Experience

Experience with a subject brings a unique richness and authenticity to your presentation that can't be replicated through mere research. When you speak from personal or professional experience, you're able to offer insights, anecdotes, and real-world examples that resonate deeply with your audience. This firsthand knowledge allows you to speak with authority and conviction, enhancing your credibility and earning the trust of your listeners. Whether you're sharing lessons learned from successes or challenges, your experiences add a valuable layer of depth and relevance to your presentation.

Practical experience enables you to navigate complexities and nuances of the subject matter with confidence. You've likely encountered various scenarios, perspectives, and outcomes related to the topic, which equips you to address different aspects comprehensively. This depth of understanding allows you to provide nuanced perspectives, practical advice, and meaningful solutions that resonate with your audience's interests and needs. It also positions you as a trusted guide who can offer valuable insights and guidance based on real-world experiences.

Sharing your experience fosters a genuine connection with your audience. By recounting personal stories or professional achievements, you humanize the information you're presenting. This authenticity not only captures the attention of your listeners but also makes your message more relatable and memorable. People are more likely to engage with and remember stories and experiences that evoke emotions or insights. Ultimately, drawing on your experience when speaking to an audience enriches your presentation, strengthens your message, and creates a lasting impact that goes beyond the words spoken. It's a powerful way to share knowledge, inspire others, and build meaningful connections in your professional and personal endeavors.

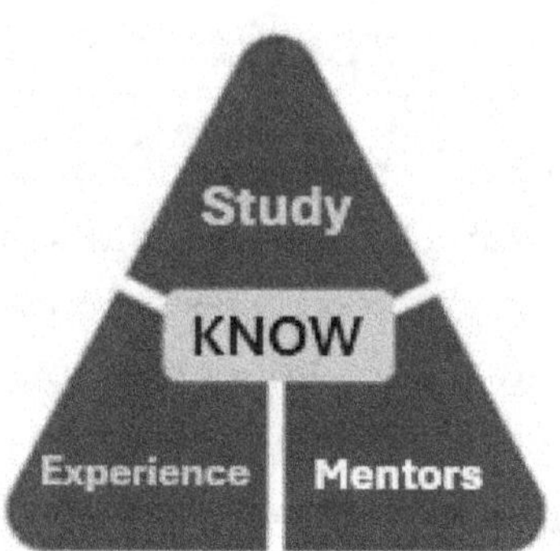
Study
KNOW
Experience
Mentors

Mentors

Having mentors to help with topics for a speaking engagement can be a game-changer in more ways than one. Firstly, mentors bring a wealth of wisdom and experience that can enrich your understanding of the subject matter. Their guidance helps you navigate complexities, gain new perspectives, and uncover valuable insights that you might not have considered on your own. Whether it's refining your message, validating your approach, or suggesting relevant examples, their input can significantly enhance the quality and depth of your presentation.

Mentors provide invaluable support and encouragement throughout the preparation process. They offer constructive feedback, helping you to fine-tune your content and delivery. Their mentorship ensures that your presentation is well-rounded, engaging, and aligned with your audience's interests and expectations. Additionally, mentors can share their own experiences and lessons learned from speaking engagements, offering practical tips and strategies for success. Their mentorship not only boosts your confidence but also equips you with the skills and knowledge to deliver a memorable and impactful presentation.

Finally, having mentors to assist with topics for a speaking engagement builds a strong network of support and collaboration. It fosters a relationship of mutual trust and respect, where you can openly discuss ideas, seek advice, and learn from each other's experiences. Mentors often have a vested interest in your success and are invested in helping you grow professionally. Their guidance extends beyond just the immediate presentation—it can contribute to your long-term development as a speaker and thought leader in your field. Ultimately, having mentors to assist with topics for speaking engagements is like having a trusted advisor by your side, guiding you towards delivering presentations that are insightful, compelling, and impactful. Their mentorship is a valuable resource that accelerates your growth and enhances your effectiveness as a communicator.

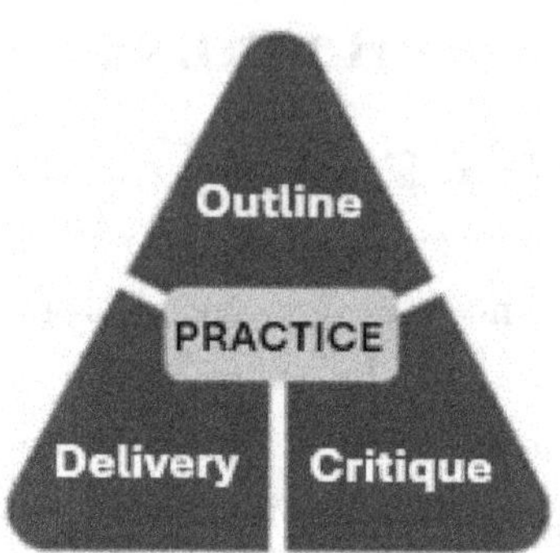
Outline
PRACTICE
Delivery
Critique

PRACTICE

There is an opinion that to be an expert at something...one needs to devote 10,000 hours of practice to that particular thing. Pro golfers, industry salespeople and public speakers are just a few examples of professions that require lots of practice. The reason for that is...it has to become second nature for you instead of "thinking while doing." Not mechanical or contrived but flowing naturally as if in a living room speaking casually.

Practicing public speaking is like honing any skill—it's essential to becoming a masterful communicator. The more you practice, the more comfortable and confident you become in front of an audience. Through practice, you refine your delivery, improve your timing, and polish your ability to convey your message effectively. This not only enhances your overall speaking skills but also allows you to handle unexpected situations with ease. Whether it's adjusting to a technical glitch or responding to audience questions, practicing prepares you to navigate challenges gracefully and maintain audience engagement.

Furthermore, consistent practice helps you to develop your own unique speaking style and voice. It allows you to experiment with different techniques, such as vocal variety, gestures, and storytelling, to find what works best for you. Each practice session builds upon the last, enabling you to identify strengths to amplify and areas for improvement to address. Over time, you become more adept at connecting with your audience, delivering impactful presentations that leave a lasting impression. Ultimately, practicing public speaking is not just about mastering the mechanics—it's about cultivating confidence, refining your skills, and continually evolving as a communicator who can captivate and inspire others with your words.

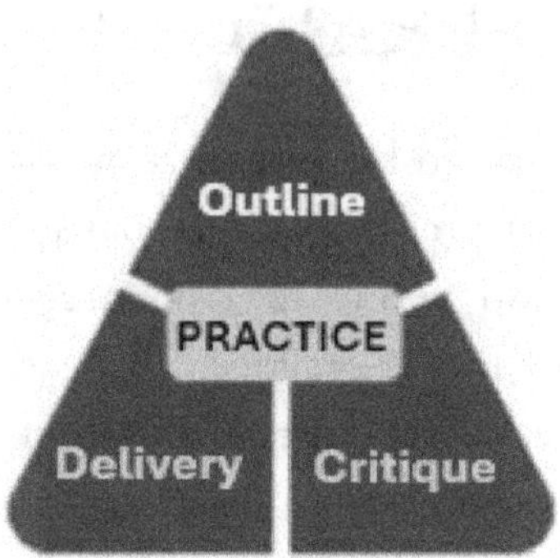
Outline
PRACTICE
Delivery
Critique

Outline

Having a good outline when preparing to make a speech is like having a roadmap—it keeps you focused, organized, and ensures your message flows smoothly. Firstly, a well-structured outline helps clarify your ideas and key points. It forces you to think critically about the content of your speech, identifying the most important information to include and the best order to present it. This clarity not only helps you stay on track during your presentation but also ensures that your audience can follow your logic and absorb your message effectively.

Secondly, a good outline serves as a framework for your speech, providing a clear structure that guides both you and your audience through the presentation. It typically includes an introduction to hook your audience and establish your topic, a body section where you delve into your main points with supporting evidence or examples, and a conclusion to summarize your key points and leave a lasting impression. This structured approach helps maintain coherence and ensures that your speech has a logical flow, making it easier for your audience to understand and retain the information you're sharing.

Thirdly, a well-crafted outline allows you to manage your time effectively during your speech. By outlining the key elements of your presentation, you can allocate time appropriately to each section, ensuring that you cover all essential points without rushing or running over your allotted time. This helps maintain audience engagement and respect for their time. Additionally, having a clear outline gives you confidence as a speaker, knowing that you have a solid plan in place to guide you through your presentation. It allows you to focus on delivering your message with clarity and conviction, knowing that you are well-prepared and organized. Ultimately, a good outline is an invaluable tool that sets the stage for a successful and impactful speech, ensuring that both you and your audience have a rewarding experience.

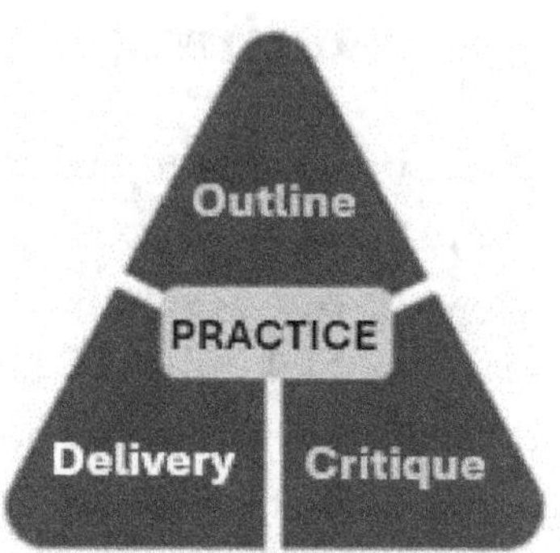

Outline
PRACTICE
Delivery
Critique

Delivery

Honing your delivery for a speech is key to effectively engaging and influencing your audience. Firstly, how you deliver your message plays a crucial role in how it is received and understood. Your delivery includes aspects such as vocal tone, pace, gestures, and body language—all of which contribute to the overall impact of your presentation. By refining these elements, you can enhance your ability to capture and maintain your audience's attention throughout your speech. A well-honed delivery not only makes your message more compelling but also ensures that it resonates with your listeners on both intellectual and emotional levels.

Practicing and honing your delivery allows you to convey confidence and authority as a speaker. Confidence is contagious, and when you speak with assurance and conviction, your audience is more likely to trust and believe in your message. This is particularly important when discussing complex or controversial topics where your credibility as a speaker is crucial. Effective delivery also includes the ability to adapt to the mood and reactions of your audience, ensuring that you can adjust your tone and approach as needed to maintain engagement and connection.

And finally, honing your delivery helps you to effectively convey the intended emotions and nuances of your speech. Whether you're aiming to inspire, persuade, educate, or entertain, your delivery style can significantly influence how your message is perceived and remembered. By practicing different techniques and refining your delivery, you can tailor your presentation to evoke the desired emotional responses from your audience. This makes your speech not only informative but also impactful and memorable. Ultimately, honing your delivery is about maximizing the effectiveness of your communication skills, ensuring that your message is not only heard but also understood, appreciated, and embraced by your audience.

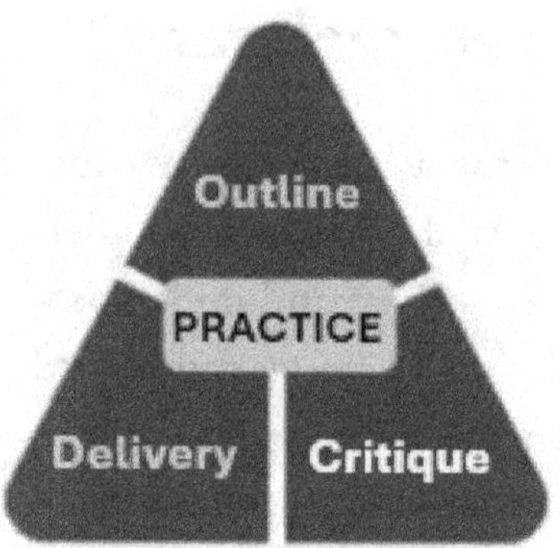

Outline
PRACTICE
Delivery
Critique

Critique

Having someone critique your speech or watching yourself on video is like having a trusted coach by your side—it's a powerful tool for continuous improvement. Firstly, feedback from others provides valuable insights that you might not notice on your own. Whether it's a mentor, colleague, or friend, their perspective can offer constructive criticism on aspects such as clarity, pacing, body language, and overall impact. This feedback helps you identify strengths to build upon and areas for improvement to address, guiding you towards refining your delivery and enhancing the effectiveness of your message.

Watching yourself on video can be an eye-opening experience. It allows you to see firsthand how you come across to others—your mannerisms, facial expressions, vocal intonation, and body language. This self-awareness is crucial for identifying habits or behaviors that may detract from your message or audience engagement. It also enables you to pinpoint moments where you shine and moments where adjustments are needed. By critically analyzing your own performance, you can make conscious efforts to improve specific aspects of your delivery and presentation style.

Receiving critiques or self-evaluating through video helps you build resilience and adaptability as a speaker. It teaches you to embrace feedback as a learning opportunity rather than a critique of your abilities. Over time, this process strengthens your confidence and ability to handle different speaking challenges with poise and effectiveness. It also fosters a growth mindset, encouraging you to continuously strive for improvement and mastery in your public speaking skills. Ultimately, seeking feedback and self-evaluation through video are essential steps in the journey towards becoming a more polished and impactful speaker. It empowers you to refine your strengths, address weaknesses, and ultimately deliver presentations that resonate deeply with your audience.

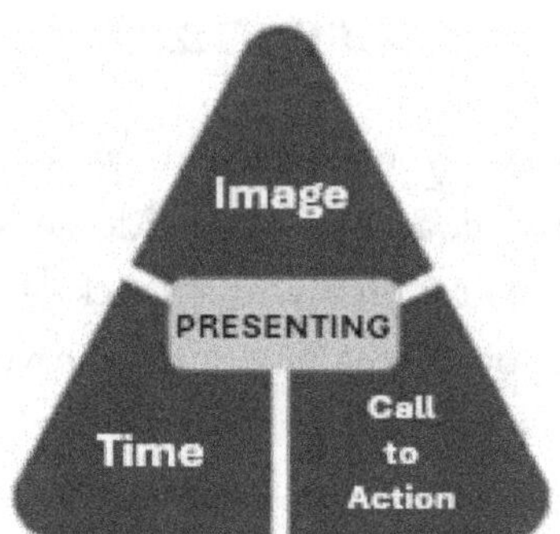
Image
PRESENTING
Time
Call
to
Action

PRESENTING

Presenting and delivering a speech successfully is both an art and a skill that can be honed with practice and preparation. Firstly, it's essential to start strong with a compelling introduction that grabs your audience's attention. This could be a thought-provoking question, a powerful quote, or a captivating story related to your topic. Engaging your audience from the outset sets the tone for the rest of your speech and ensures they are eager to hear more.

Pacing is crucial in maintaining audience interest throughout your presentation. Varying your pace helps to emphasize key points, maintain momentum, and prevent monotony. It's important to speak clearly and audibly, allowing your words to resonate with your audience. Additionally, incorporating pauses at strategic moments can add emphasis, allow your audience to digest important information, and create a sense of anticipation.

Then, effective body language and gestures can significantly enhance your delivery. Your non-verbal communication, such as facial expressions, gestures, and posture, conveys confidence, enthusiasm, and conviction. Maintaining eye contact with your audience establishes a connection and shows sincerity. Using gestures to illustrate key points can make your speech more dynamic and visually engaging. When your body language aligns with your message, it reinforces your credibility and helps to convey your message more effectively.

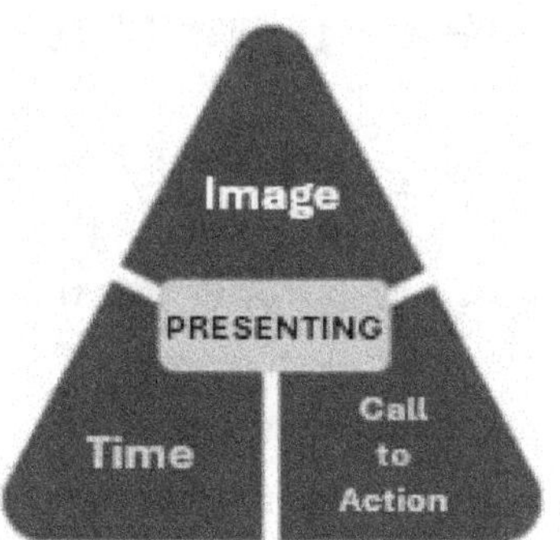
Image
PRESENTING
Time
Call
to
Action

Image

Having a good image when delivering a speech goes beyond just appearance—it encompasses how you present yourself holistically to your audience. Firstly, your attire and grooming play a role in creating a positive first impression. Dressing appropriately for the occasion shows respect for your audience and the importance of the event. When you look polished and put-together, it enhances your credibility and professionalism as a speaker. It also sets the tone for how seriously your audience will take your message.

Body language and demeanor contribute significantly to your image as a speaker. Your posture, gestures, and facial expressions should convey confidence, enthusiasm, and sincerity. Maintaining good posture shows that you are attentive and engaged, while expressive gestures can emphasize key points and make your speech more dynamic. Facial expressions that reflect your emotions and convey empathy can help you connect with your audience on a deeper level. These non-verbal cues reinforce the authenticity of your message and enhance your overall image as a speaker.

The tone and quality of your voice are crucial aspects of your image when delivering a speech. A clear, modulated voice that is audible and articulate ensures that your message is heard and understood by everyone in the audience. Varying your vocal tone and pace can add emphasis, maintain interest, and convey different emotions or moods within your speech. Additionally, speaking with enthusiasm and conviction demonstrates your passion for the topic and captures the attention of your listeners. When your voice is well-controlled and expressive, it enhances your authority and persuasiveness as a speaker.

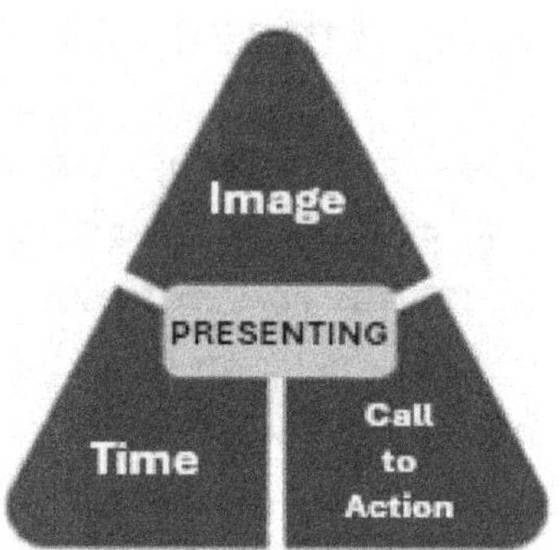
Image
PRESENTING
Time
Call
to
Action

Time

Being mindful of your time when speaking to an audience is crucial for several reasons. Firstly, respecting the allotted time shows consideration for your audience's schedule and attention span. People have busy lives, and when you adhere to the agreed-upon timeframe, you demonstrate professionalism and respect for their time. It also ensures that your audience remains engaged and attentive throughout your speech, as they are more likely to absorb and retain information when it's delivered within a reasonable timeframe.

Effective time management allows you to deliver a well-structured and coherent presentation. When you plan your speech with a designated timeframe in mind, you can organize your content effectively, prioritize key points, and allocate sufficient time to each section. This prevents you from rushing through important information or running over the allotted time, which can lead to confusion or frustration among your audience. A well-paced presentation enhances clarity and comprehension, making it easier for your audience to follow your message and grasp the significance of your ideas.

Finally, being mindful of your time demonstrates your proficiency and mastery as a speaker. It showcases your ability to communicate succinctly and effectively, conveying your message with clarity and precision. By delivering a concise and impactful presentation, you leave a positive impression on your audience and enhance your reputation as a competent and considerate speaker. Ultimately, being mindful of your time not only enhances the quality of your speech but also reflects your professionalism and commitment to delivering a valuable and memorable presentation.

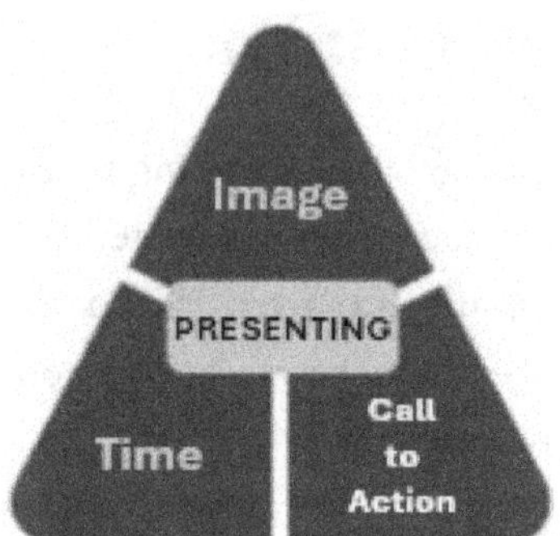

Image
PRESENTING
Time
Call
to
Action

Call to Action

As your speech nears its conclusion, calling for action is a powerful way to leave a lasting impact on your audience. Firstly, it provides clear direction for your listeners on what they should do next or how they can apply the information you've shared. Whether it's encouraging them to take specific steps, adopt new practices, or consider a different perspective, a call to action motivates your audience to translate your words into meaningful actions. This not only reinforces the relevance and importance of your message but also empowers your audience to initiate positive change in their own lives or communities.

A well-crafted call to action helps to reinforce the key points of your speech and solidify your message in the minds of your audience. By summarizing your main ideas and emphasizing their significance, you underscore the relevance of your message and its potential impact. This reinforcement aids in retention and encourages deeper reflection on the insights or solutions you've presented. A compelling call to action inspires your audience to consider how they can contribute to achieving shared goals or addressing challenges discussed during your speech.

Calling for action fosters engagement and involvement from your audience beyond the confines of your presentation. It encourages them to become active participants in the topics or issues you've addressed, sparking discussions, initiatives, or collaborations. This engagement extends the reach and influence of your message, creating ripple effects that can lead to broader awareness, advocacy, or positive change. By motivating your audience to take action, you transform passive listeners into motivated individuals who are inspired to make a difference in their own spheres of influence. Ultimately, a strong call to action not only concludes your speech on a compelling note but also empowers your audience to become agents of change and catalysts for progress.

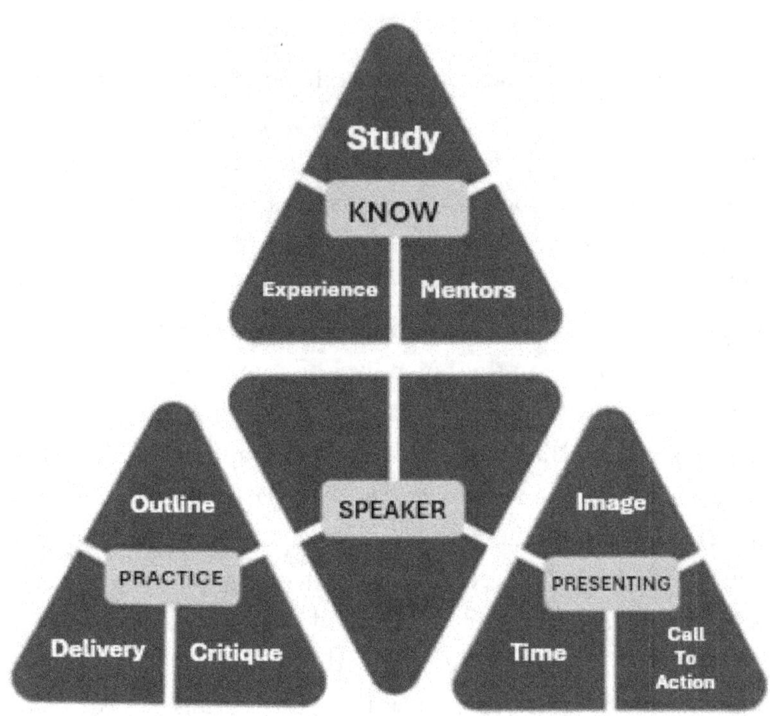
Study
KNOW
Experience
Mentors
SPEAKER
Outline
PRACTICE
Delivery
Critique
Image
PRESENTING
Time
Call
To
Action

Bonus Chapter – Joining a Speaker Club

Joining a speaker's club can be a fantastic way to hone your communication skills and boost your confidence in a supportive environment. These clubs, like Toastmasters International or local public speaking groups, provide a structured platform where members can practice speaking, receive constructive feedback, and continuously improve. Imagine stepping into a room where everyone is there to help you shine—not judge your every word but cheer you on as you grow!

Firstly, speaker's clubs offer a safe space to experiment with different speaking styles and techniques. Whether you're tackling prepared speeches, impromptu talks, or even leading meetings, you'll find ample opportunities to stretch your abilities. Each time you speak, you'll receive constructive evaluations from fellow members who want to see you succeed. This feedback loop is invaluable for pinpointing areas to refine and strengths to celebrate. It's like having a team of coaches dedicated to helping you become the best speaker you can be!

Secondly, the networking opportunities within speaker's clubs are golden. You'll meet people from diverse backgrounds and professions, all united by a passion for effective communication. These connections can lead to mentorship opportunities, collaborations on projects, or simply friendships with like-minded individuals. Plus, sharing your journey with others who understand your goals creates a supportive community where you can learn from each other's experiences and insights.

Lastly, joining a speaker's club is a gateway to personal growth. Overcoming the fear of public speaking is often cited as one of the top fears for many people, and by confronting it head-on in a friendly, encouraging environment, you'll build resilience and self-assurance. As you progress in your speaking abilities, you'll notice improvements in your everyday interactions, from meetings at work to social gatherings. The skills you develop—articulating ideas clearly, engaging an audience, and thinking on your feet—are invaluable in both professional and personal spheres. So, don't hesitate to take that leap and join a speaker's club. It's not just about becoming a better speaker—it's about becoming a more confident, empowered communicator overall!

SUMMARY

Joining a speakers' bureau can be a highly beneficial strategy for honing your speaking skills and expanding your professional network. Firstly, speakers' bureaus connect speakers with opportunities to present at various events, conferences, and gatherings. This exposure not only provides valuable practice in front of diverse audiences but also allows you to refine your presentation style and adapt to different speaking environments. Each speaking engagement offers a chance to learn and grow as a speaker, gaining confidence and experience along the way.

Secondly, being part of a speakers' bureau enhances your visibility within your industry or community. Bureaus often promote their speakers through their networks and platforms, increasing your chances of being recognized and sought after for speaking engagements. This exposure can lead to networking opportunities with other professionals, potential clients, or collaborators who attend or organize these events. Building relationships through speaking engagements can open doors to new partnerships, referrals, and career advancements.

Thirdly, speakers' bureaus provide valuable support and resources to help you succeed. They often offer training, coaching, and feedback to improve your speaking skills and enhance your presentation materials. Additionally, bureaus may provide logistical support, such as handling event bookings, negotiating fees, and managing travel arrangements, allowing you to focus more on delivering impactful presentations. By leveraging the resources and opportunities offered by a speakers' bureau, you can accelerate your growth as a speaker, expand your influence, and build a reputation as a trusted and sought-after presenter in your field.

Invitation

When I got into public speaking some 50 years ago, I had a veteran speaker tell me this "Don, just get up there and 1) tell 'em *what you're going to tell 'em*' then 2) '*tell 'em*' and finally 3) tell 'em *what you just told 'em*'." As simple as those instructions were...it was very helpful as I grew in the business.

Today, we have more sophisticated tools to work with and that's my suggestion here. Do whatever works for you. Watch videos on YouTube. Follow great speakers on the circuit. Get involved with a group that does public speaking for lots of practice.

Who knows...you might be a natural or it might be stage fright that makes it difficult. I personally had a blast speaking over the years because I made sure to stick with what I knew. Salesmanship, parenting and golf were typically my topics. By sticking to my expertise, I was comfortable just getting up and speaking from the heart.

Some of the best speakers I heard over the years...and I heard hundreds of them, were very down-to-earth in their style. It was just natural for them to be up there, and they were speaking from experience...not a "canned speech." Nobody cared if their English wasn't proper or that their mannerisms were awkward. It was easy to get caught in their presentations because they were genuine and really new what they were talking about.

So, what can we take from this experience? Be as real and natural as you can be. The audience will love it and you!

When you're with someone who is sharing their struggles with you...just smile at him/her and give them one of these. He/she will ask "What is that?" Then simply reply "Life Works in Threes."

Other titles coming out:

- Weight Struggles?
- Abundance Struggles?
- Parenting Struggles?
- Life Struggles?
- Purpose Struggles?
- Happiness Struggles?
- Sales Struggles?
- Romance Struggles?
- Time Struggles?
- Network Struggles?
- Marriage Struggles?
- Divorce Struggles?
- Money Struggles?
- Career Struggles?
- Dating Struggles?
- Caretaker Struggles?
- Forgiveness Struggles?
- Grieving Struggles?
- Success Struggles?
- Golf Struggles?
- Workplace Struggles?
- Stress Struggles?
- Shame/Guilt Struggles?
- Addiction Struggles?

Quotes about Speakership

"All the great speakers were bad speakers at first." - Ralph Waldo Emerson

"The human brain starts working the moment you are born and never stops until you stand up to speak in public." - George Jessel

"Public speaking is the art of diluting a two-minute idea with a two-hour vocabulary." - John F. Kennedy

"If you can't explain it simply, you don't understand it well enough." - Albert Einstein

"There are always three speeches, for everyone you actually gave. The one you practiced, the one you gave, and the one you wish you gave." - Dale Carnegie

Public speaking topics that typically resonate well with audiences often revolve around issues that are relevant, engaging, and impactful. Here are some popular topics that audiences generally find interesting:

1. **Personal Development and Motivation**:
   - Goal setting and achievement
   - Overcoming adversity
   - Building resilience
   - Time management and productivity
2. **Technology and Innovation**:
   - The future of [industry]
   - Artificial intelligence and its implications
   - Cybersecurity and data privacy
   - Ethical implications of technology
3. **Health and Wellness**:
   - Mental health awareness
   - Nutrition and fitness
   - Stress management
   - Aging and longevity
4. **Environmental Issues**:
   - Climate change and sustainability
   - Conservation efforts
   - Renewable energy solutions
   - Eco-friendly lifestyles
5. **Social Issues**:
   - Diversity, equity, and inclusion

- ○ Human rights and activism
- ○ Social justice movements
- ○ Poverty alleviation and economic development

6. **Career and Professional Development:**
   - ○ Leadership skills
   - ○ Networking strategies
   - ○ Effective communication in the workplace
   - ○ Entrepreneurship and startups

7. **Current Events and Politics:**
   - ○ Global trends and geopolitics
   - ○ Political polarization and its impact
   - ○ Crisis management and conflict resolution
   - ○ International relations and diplomacy

8. **Education and Learning:**
   - ○ The future of education
   - ○ Lifelong learning and continuous improvement
   - ○ Educational technology (EdTech)
   - ○ Innovations in teaching and learning methods

9. **Entertainment and Pop Culture:**
   - ○ Impact of media on society
   - ○ Trends in popular culture
   - ○ Celebrity influence
   - ○ Evolution of entertainment industries

10. **History and Culture:**
    - ○ Cultural diversity and heritage

      preservation
- Lessons from historical events
- Archaeological discoveries
- Influence of ancient civilizations on modern society

When selecting a topic, consider your audience's interests, the relevance of the subject matter, and how you can deliver a message that resonates emotionally or intellectually with them. Additionally, tailoring your speech to address current issues or trends can enhance engagement and relevance.

Remember,

When you get right down to it,

Life is about making choices.

Every day, all day long, that's what we do.

- *We choose to get out of bed or not.*
- *We choose to clean up or not.*
- *We choose what to eat all day.*
- *We choose to exercise or not.*
- *We choose to go to work or not.*
- *We choose to do a good job or not.*
- *We choose to come home or not.*
- *We choose to watch TV or do something constructive.*
- *We choose to bed at a decent hour or not.*

And the next day...we start all over again.

What is the meaning of this? Get good at choosing.

Before you can get good at choosing though...you need to understand how life works in threes.

Best speaking advice, I ever got from a pro speaker -

"Tell 'em what you're going to tell 'em.
Then, tell 'em.
And then, tell 'em what you just told 'em."

When someone is struggling with a particular area or two, chances are they are "out of balance" with how life works. How does life work? Life works in threes.

If you're interested in personal topics like life, health, money or business topics like sales, time management and public speaking...TRYUNE WORKS! can shed some light on creating success in those areas.

The definition of TRIUNE is a group of three things; united. Being three in one, such as - humans are *mental, physical* and *spiritual beings.* The word TRYUNE is a play of the word TRIUNE, encouraging all to try this concept and help eliminate struggling unnecessarily.

LifeWorksInThrees.com